T0088387

DAVID BEDNALL

EVOCATION OF WELLS CATHEDRAL

MUSIC DEPARTMENT

OXFORD
UNIVERSITY PRESS

for Elsa van der Zee
with much love and gratitude, and in tribute to her knowledge and love of Wells Cathedral, particularly the Jesse Window

Evocation of Wells Cathedral

'O Radix Jesse'

DAVID BEDNALL

Slow and mysterious

pp **Sw. Flute 8'**

5

9

cresc.

14

dim.

pp

© Oxford University Press 2019

Printed in Great Britain

OXFORD UNIVERSITY PRESS, MUSIC DEPARTMENT, GREAT CLARENDON STREET, OXFORD OX2 6DP
The Moral Rights of the Composer have been asserted. Photocopying this copyright material is ILLEGAL.

* Wherever possible the second line down should be played on a clarinet or cromorne. If preferred simply incorporate it into the top line.

36
Gt.
legato
Pushing forwards slightly
40
Gt. + Sw. Foundations 8',
Sw. + Hautbois
mf sonore e legato
+ Gt.
mf sonore
44
48

Sempre incalzando
+ Flutes 4'
52
+ Foundations 4'
56
+ Swell Reeds 8' (Box closed)
60
rit.
+ Foundations 16'
+ Swell Reeds 16', 4'
64

Molto maestoso
68
molto f e sonore
Sw. - Reeds 16', 4'
- Foundations 16'
72
Foundations 8', Flutes 4'
76
Foundations 8'
80
Cornet
Soft Foundations 8'
mp legato

Clifton Village, 28 July 2016